Table of Contents

EMOTIONAL INTELLIGENCE

*How to Use Emotions to Improve Self-Awareness,
Develop Social Skills, Communicate Effectively,
Empathize with Others, and Defuse Conflict.
A Practical Guide for Success*

Richard Campbell and Emma Parker

Emotional intelligence sounds like something big and complicated, but it really is just the ability to identify emotions, both yours and those of other people. This basic skill can be a segue to enhance and improve all areas of your life both internally to regulate your own emotions as well as with your relationships with family, friends, and co-workers. A person who is in touch with their emotions can make better choices regarding their actions and avoid poor decisions based on elevated emotions. Getting in touch with your emotions can also help you understand the emotions of others, and thus, you are equipped to navigate life situations more easily and with less conflict.

Improving your emotional intelligence does not mean that you must always appear happy or even in control, but it does mean that you can tell when you are becoming upset about something or sad and can identify your behavioral tendencies based on your emotions. In addition, knowing how emotions make you feel can help you empathize with others based on their emotions.

Sometimes a sign of emotional intelligence can be a simple pause. For example, you receive criticism about how a paper you handed in for an assignment at work or school. Your first impulse may be to get upset, shove the paper in your notebook, and stomp off feeling a mixture of shame and the state of being unappreciated. However, a more productive course of action is to talk to your teacher or co-worker about what they didn't like about your work so you can better understand their expectations. Remember, this will not be your last assignment, so remaining calm and taking a close look at where your errors are can help you to improve your performance and do better next time. Also, becoming upset and not communicating does nothing positive for your relationship with the co-worker or teacher. By using emotional intelligence and learning from the situation, you strengthen relationships, and your reputation with each person is increased.

Chapter 1:
What is Emotional Intelligence?

Let's explain emotional intelligence with examples of how it can help your life increasing your happiness, improving your relationships as well as how to get through situations where the other person is not applying emotional intelligence.

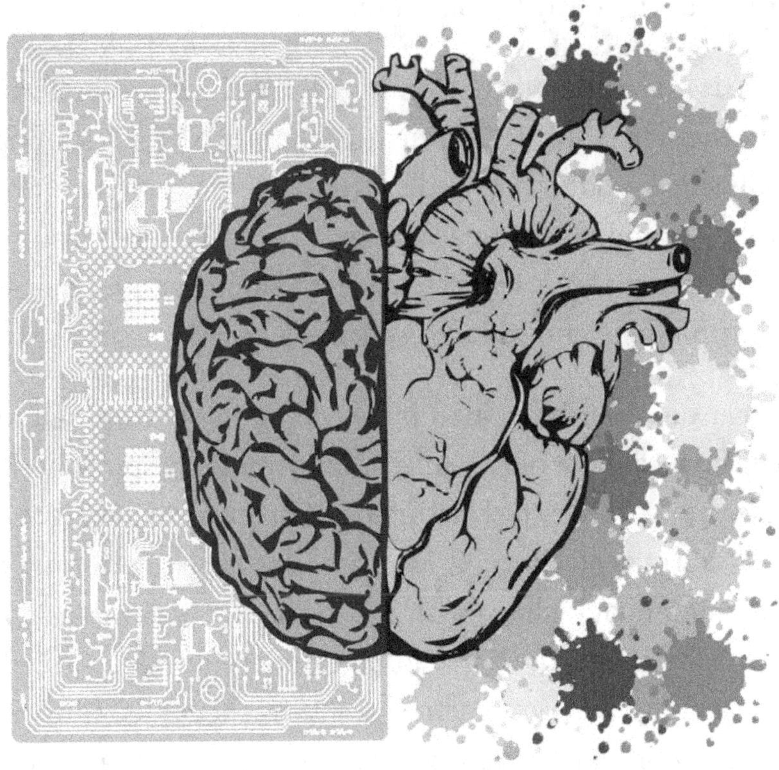

As simple as it sounds, it can be quite difficult to apply. Emotional intelligence is the ability to be self-aware. It implies that you to know what you are feeling, understand your emotions, and also know how your emotions can affect other people. You know how to manage your own emotions without becoming overly upset in the wrong setting and making things more difficult than they have to be. A person with these abilities can also have a very positive impact on other people's emotions. Remaining calm lessens the potential for others to become upset. The calmest person in the room generally has the reigns. It really is true that a person is never so powerless as when he is upset and arguing with others as a way to communicate.

There is an argument that emotional intelligence is inherited but whether nature or nurture the tools for emotional intelligence can be practiced and applied in everyday life and it will definitely have a good impact on every relationship in life including those with colleagues, employers, employees, and with family and romantic partners.

A great deal can be gained by checking in with oneself and being honest about our feelings. Has something someone said made you feel angry or frustrated? When we are having these lower vibration feelings, it is very easy to become short with your answers and sharp with your words. However, a much more helpful approach would be to pause and acknowledge those feelings without reacting or letting them take control of our behavior. By acknowledging our feelings, we are letting ourselves be heard internally, and we understand why our pulse may go up, and it's easy to get into an argument at that point. However, by taking a little time for ourselves and focusing on our breath, we can keep our emotions in check and thus taken control of a situation instead of letting it control us.

When we are frustrated or angry, it can be hard to remember empathy. It can be helpful to look at the other person and practice really seeing them. You should now approach the situation fully, believing that the other person has good intentions. Remember who this person is and their relationship to you. This can help to relieve your stress enough to proceed in a positive way.

First, visualize the situation from the other person's perspective. It is highly likely that their emotions are similar to yours right now. If you are frustrated, it's likely that they are too, and they are likely nervous and apprehensive about your reaction just as you may be feeling the same. For example, someone who works for you comes to you to tell you that while they had agreed to have made ten copies of booklets and bound them for your upcoming meeting tomorrow, the project is running late. You may initially be angry, and perhaps your first impulse is to become grouchy, asking them why and complaining about how that will put you behind.

This is the moment to take a pause and focus on your breathing, remembering that this is your employee and that their performance is generally good and on time. Understand that they must be feeling nervous about coming to you with this news and would prefer to please you with a project coming in on time. Perhaps instead, try to gain an understanding of why the project will be late. There may be a piece of equipment or program that is inhibiting their progress. By taking this approach, your employee will feel less anxiety and will likely open up to you and tell you that the copy machine keeps jamming up, and they have had to open up the machine and pull out the crumpled paper several times. As this person's manager, you need to remember that it is your job to remove roadblocks from their path to success.

Using this process, you have just empathized with your employee and applied social skills remembering the nature of your relationship with your employee. Perhaps you suggest that your employee go down to Office Depot and give him some money from petty cash to complete the project of copying and binding the booklets this afternoon so they will be ready for tomorrow's meeting. Suggest that when they return, they can call the repair shop and ask them to come and have a look at the copy machine so that this doesn't happen in the future.

Actually, in this situation, you might congratulate your employee for the self-motivation it took for him to proactively come to you with the problem. If you think about it, instead of continuing to try to put the booklets together and elongating the process without success, he showed leadership qualities by being honest. He got out ahead of the situation and let you know he had a problem with time for a course correction. This actually makes him a very valuable employee, and instead of allowing yourself to behave poorly and demotivate him, you have strengthened your relationship and demonstrated what it means to be a good leader. You have turned what could have made for a stressful work environment, which would probably lead to your employee finding other work causing turnover in the workplace for you and require you to train someone else.

In this example, the boss in question has exhibited very strong emotional intelligence and improved the work environment. S/he empathized with the employee, used breathing techniques to keep their response measured and used a potential conflict as a teaching moment on how a leader conducts himself/herself in the face of a problem. The work environment will be strengthened in a positive way, and this employee will remember this event and very likely will talk about it to others in the organization and the community.

In this book, we are going to go into depth about tools that can be employed to improve one's "EQ." By practicing, we can improve our relationships, and these more helpful practices will become our habit patterns.

There are five components of emotional intelligence, which we will be discussing in their respective order throughout the course of the book- self-awareness, self-regulation, social skills, empathy, and motivation. Emotional intelligence means understanding other people as well as yourself. In fact, we will be talking about the aspects that are directed at the self first because if you don't know yourself, you can't connect with anyone else. Everyone could get in better touch with themselves.

The first step to self-improvement is to figure out what needs to be improved. This doesn't mean beat yourself up about it. This is not a time to hold your flaws over your head. That is actually something known as negative self-talk, which is completely unproductive. You only tear yourself down and never get to the point where you build yourself up. People who do not feel a sense of self-worth are unlikely to try to self-improve because they do not think they can do so. It becomes a mixture of beating yourself down and throwing a pity party. When you recognize your flaws with clarity and look at them with neutrality, you have achieved self-awareness. Self-awareness means being completely honest, both with yourself and with other people.

Self-regulation is about being in control of your emotions instead of the other way around. You recognize how you are feeling, but you decide you are not going to be overcome by it and create your own outcome. You say to yourself, "I know I am feeling this way now, and it is an unpleasant feeling, but that is going to pass. I need to make my decisions based on the truth."

Social skills are about navigating through the complex web that is human interaction. This is often portrayed by media about being witty, "cool," and having a persona that other people will find attractive. It is more about taking your own unique personality and using it to be the most positive, friendly, and open version of yourself.

Empathy is caring for and understanding others. However, this does not mean changing your opinions based on what other people say. The best type of leader listens to what everyone on their team has to say and makes a decision that takes all of these opinions, along with their own into consideration. The best type of friend reaches out to understand where the other person is coming from while still standing their ground.

Motivation is basically your internal drive. It is what makes you get out of bed in the morning. Whatever you spend the most time doing is where your motivations lie, and that is why you need to make sure what motivates you is something good.

Everything we do is out of motivation, and that is a fact that emotionally intelligent people are willing to accept and in fact, use to their advantage. It is easy to slip into the mentality that we do what we have to do and that the circumstances and actions of the people around us have total control over us.

For example, you've probably heard someone say, "That person insulted me. I had to insult them back!" It might sound logical when they explain that they would have come off looking like a coward if they did not "step up to the plate" and engage in an argument with the other person. However, the truth is that no one can make anyone look a certain way. Our actions make statements only about our own selves and no one else. The actions of someone else do not set up a requirement for you to do something. In fact, if you think about it, the greatest retort to an insult is silence. This is showing the other person that their insult is not worthy of a reply. You will come out looking like the mature one while they come across as petty.

What the goal is when you are searching for yourself is to figure out what needs to be worked on. Everyone is a work in progress. Think about when an invention is introduced, and a flaw in its inner workings is noticed. This doesn't mean the product is not a good one and needs to be tossed out. In fact, that means it has so much potential that it is worth working on. Think of it that way when you are working on yourself. You have endless potential, and you are overall a good person. Just because you do things that are wrong, does not mean you are a bad person. The fact that you know when you have done something wrong actually means you are good. It also means you are already practicing self-awareness. If you were a "bad" person, you would not question the morals of what you were doing, and if you did know what you were doing was wrong, there wouldn't be any conflict inside of you about it.

Let's say your flaw is that you are too quick to anger. This does not cancel out the good things about you, nor does it mean your episodes of anger are born out of evil within you. It is a personality flaw, and we all have them. Having admitted to this problem is completing the first step, which is being self-aware enough to know yourself.

There is a misconception that emotionally intelligent people do not feel negative emotions or have poor reactions to anything. They have the same human reactions as everyone else does, but they handle their emotions in a constructive way. They pause before reacting, recognizing that the first response one thinks of when hit with news they did not want to hear is probably not a good course of action. They recognize the feelings they are experiencing, even the negative ones, and they figure out what would be better ways to express them. If they do have a poor reaction to something, they apologize to whoever they need to.

Over the course of this book, you will learn how to get more in touch with yourself and to be the one in charge of your emotions. Emotions are powerful beings and can make you feel like you do not have any influence over them. This is not true. Emotions are messages our brains send as a means of trying to interpret the events that happen around us so that we can gain a better understanding of the world we live in. They come and go, and they are not always accurate. They should not be seen as entities that have power over us.

An emotionally intelligent person does not always know what to do, but they are open to learning what behavior is acceptable for each individual situation. Etiquette and the right thing to do are not general concepts to where one method can be applied to every person or situation. You have to take situations on a case-by-case basis and figure out what this particular circumstance calls. That is true emotional intelligence, being flexible and adaptable.

A leader has to learn what motivates each individual person. Some people need gentle coaxing. Others only respond to "tough love." Some people need to be praised for their work in order to stay motivated to keep going. Others need what is sometimes referred to as dark motivation. This means they need to be pushed with threats of consequences they could suffer for not completing the tasks they need to. For example, if they are simply told, "you need to have this assignment handed in by the end of the week," it is not guaranteed that they will do what you ask of them. If you try to give them a friendly reminder, it will be shrugged off. You have to tell them if they do not do this assignment, their grades or position in the firm will suffer. For a gentle person, this will not come naturally, but there are some people you will need to do this with. They will not listen to you any other way. You will probably work with people like this. They might even be under your employment.

The great thing about emotional intelligence is that you do not have to change your personality. You just need to adopt healthier habits and work on getting rid of the unhealthier ones. However, emotional intelligence does not represent one personality type, nor does it condemn others. For example, if you are an introverted person, you do not have to try to convert yourself into an extroverted one. There are many successful introverted people. However, this does not mean you can get away from interacting with other people. If you want to get ahead in your career, you will need to be in contact with people on a regular basis. There will be social events you will need to attend and interact with other people. This is difficult for an introverted person because while an extroverted person gets their energy from interacting with others, it drains energy from an introvert. You will need to find time to recharge in between events. Make sure you practice self-care more than usual and have some alone time. Some introverts even find times to excuse themselves during these social events. They go to the restroom or any other place that offers a moment of privacy. This is where they can collect themselves. They might just stand there for a moment, or there might be some sort of ritual they have that helps them regain composure. This could include listening to music, repeating a mantra, or anything else the individual finds to be calming.

You might compare yourself to people who are known for being charismatic, whether they are celebrities are the more popular people in your school or work environment, and become discouraged about your own prospects of social and career-related success. Do not write off your own talents and how they could contribute to a successful life. Put charisma and wit out of your mind for a little while.

Think about other strengths you might have, ones that make you better able to communicate with and understand others. Maybe you are good at having compassion for other people, and when they tell you a story about an unpleasant experience they have had, you conjure up the emotional or and even to some extent, physical sensations the other person might have felt. This might seem like a hindrance you have to bear, and you may wish it away, but do not underestimate the benefits this personality trait might have in store for you. A high level of compassion can be a valuable asset to a leader. People in leadership positions need to be able to connect with those under their supervision on an emotional level. If they can do this, they will be seen as likable by others, which will make them more inclined to accept their leadership over them. People want to know that someone who is making management decisions about them has their best interests at heart. For instance, a college professor has a student who usually excels in the classroom and hands in their work on time. Suddenly, the student is missing class and doing poorly on their assignments. Instead of becoming annoyed with the student, the professor sees that this is not their normal behavior, and therefore, there must be some kind of explanation. They decide to pull them aside after class and ask them if they are having some kind of personal problem that is hindering their ability to work, and in this conversation, they find out their student's mother is going through a health crisis. Now that the professor knows what the problem is, they set up a way to work with the student, giving them extensions on their deadlines and extra credit opportunities. If they had just assumed the student had become disengaged in the class, there is a possibility that this person would be facing a failing grade in their class on top of being worried about their mother (not to mention failing grades in a class look bad for the person who teaches it.) However, since the professor channeled their compassion, there is a brighter future for both of them, and the student will look back on them fondly for giving them a break when they needed it.

Along with creating a better self, using emotional intelligence can repair relationships that seem to be headed for certain doom. Many times, problems in our relationships stem from poor communication. This means both parties are not hearing one another out. This leaves people feeling like the other person does not care about what they have to say. This is going to be challenging at first if your relationship has fallen into a rut. Bad communication habits do not develop overnight, so they are not solved overnight. The unhealthy form of communication has become your natural way of interacting with one another. There is also a lack of trust between the two parties.

If you want to use emotional intelligence to salvage a relationship that has been suffering, you will need to do a certain amount of "sucking it up." When communication has been poor, there has been a lot of playing the blame game between both parties. You might feel angry at them, and there may be parts of you that feel like they are the one who is responsible for the initial conflict, but at some point, you will need to come to a decision. You will have to decide what is more important to you, saving the relationship or being the one in the right. If what you value more is your relationship, you will need to be the one to lay your weapons down first. Ask them what you can do for them to make things easier for them today. Make them something for breakfast or bring them coffee. Be cordial with them, and do not talk about the problems in your relationship. This does not mean you need to make a grand gesture. In fact, that is how the cycle of a toxic relationship goes. There are lavish gifts and declarations of love after a fight. A grand gesture only lasts a moment. What really counts is how you act on the day-to-day. Do little acts of kindness and take steps to not make the conversation go south.

Be prepared when you do this. As we talked about before, with frequent conflict comes a feeling of distrust. They are likely to question your motives if you are suddenly kind to them after there has been discord between you for a long time. They might think this is some kind of trick. This means you will need to be consistent in being kinder to them even when you are not getting the desired results. That is difficult for anyone. People naturally want quick gratification. You can help yourself overcome the frustration this comes with by just thinking about today. Do not overwhelm yourself by thinking about all of the progress that needs to be made to get your relationship back on track. Just think about having a good morning. When you manage to have a good morning, that mood might just roll over into the afternoon. Before you know it, the evening will come, and then you will have had an entirely good day. This will beget another one. This is how relationships repair. You spend some good times together. This will make you remember how things used to be and where they could be again. When you have mastered emotional intelligence, your friendships and relationships optimize.

With this advice comes a caveat. If your relationship has become violent- they hit, kick, break your things, or commit any other act that is supposed to bring harm to you, this is abuse, and you need to leave this relationship. The same goes for if they are constantly putting you down and trying to sabotage your self-esteem.

When it comes to beginning the practice of emotional intelligence, there is one extremely important rule. You will never be able to fix a problem if you do not recognize that it is there. It is no easy task to get to know yourself, and not every part of this journey will be pleasant, but it will be rewarding. For example, if you are shy and have a hard time in social situations, imagine if you were able to overcome that. That day is closer than you think. It all starts with coming to terms with the source of your shyness. Maybe that was the personality of your other family members. Maybe you did not feel comfortable speaking up in your earlier life. We can love the people we grew up with while still recognizing the mistakes that were made in your upbringing. In fact, it is a healthy way to look at your situation. Denying your emotions and experiences will do nothing except make the problem bigger than it has to be. When you recognize a negative emotion, a portion of the intensity will actually be alleviated because you are now facing the problem head-on.

Chapter 2:
Self Awareness

A person who is self-aware can understand how others perceive their actions. They know that how they behave in response to social situations relates to how others see them and that how they relate to others can either improve or diminish their reputation and relationships.

Most of us consider ourselves self-aware but don't be too quick to dismiss this critical part of emotional intelligence. One cannot develop his/her emotional intelligence without a close examination of self. Recognizing how you feel about something is easier to do in retrospect or looking into the future than it is on the fly. That's why sometimes our emotions can surprise us. We don't always know what we feel until it comes out too harshly. That is what happens when you do not stay in touch with your emotions, or write them off and repress them when you have them.

There are tools we can use to hone our abilities in self-awareness. We might keep a journal of our emotions, perhaps for a full week or other predetermined amount of time. Write about significant events that happen during the day at work, at home, at school, and at church or in any other social situation. As you consider what happened, think about your emotions as each action unfolded.

Think about the roles that you play in the lives of each of the people that you interact with regularly. Your roles might include student, teacher, spouse, parent, child, employee or employer, and likely many others. In each of these relationships, things happen often that can bring up various emotions for us, both negative and positive.

By taking inventory of our relationships and emotions that they can stimulate for us, we can assess ourselves and discover more about our abilities and strengths as well as about areas for improvement within ourselves. There is a misconception that it takes a big crisis to reveal a person's true character. However, your character comes out in daily events and little moments. These times that seem mundane or not important on a grand scale can prove to be defining moments.

One example of a daily event could be that you are racing around getting ready for work and running late when your child comes back into the house to tell you that s/he has missed the bus for school. Your first impulse might be feelings of anger because it will add an additional thing to do this morning before you get to work. Perhaps you had hoped to arrive early and get a cup of cappuccino and a crescent from the deli in the lobby of your building. By recognizing that this has piqued anger in yourself, you can realize that you now have a choice. You can succumb to the anger and grumble about, making your child feel worse about missing the bus than they already do which could result in a small wedge between you that may not last long, but it will impact how they feel the next time they need to give you bad news. In this respect, your own behavior can create a tendency in your child to conceal things from you because they know you will lose control of your anger.

The way you react to unpleasant situations is important, but especially if you are a parent. When you lose your temper with a friend or colleague, it does not impact them the way it will your own child. This is because they do not live with you. You are not raising them. You do not hold their livelihood in your hands. The way you act does not set an example for them about how people should be. When you have a child, you are teaching them about the world. You are showing them what to expect out of people and how they deserve to be treated. When we are young, we can afford to lash out in anger when a problem comes along. When we get older and are responsible for someone else's life, that is no longer an option. You need to make decisions that are good for them.

Let's go back to the scenario before. Alternatively, you might instead hear the news that your child has missed the bus and listen to him/her, taking a deep breath, letting it out slowly. This is not a huge intake of air that will automatically reveal your irritation. Use controlled breathing. You have a choice to make here, and one that will start your day better would be to smile. Let is sink in that you now have more time with your child. Slow down and think about the tasks you had laid out before you. Are there some that can be crossed off your list and replaced with this newfound extra family time? Perhaps you don't have to curl your hair this morning and drop off the dry cleaning. Perhaps instead, you can take your child to the donut shop down the street and eat with him/her, having some coffee instead of your planned cappuccino. Tell him/her that you are happy to have the unexpected time with them this morning. Maybe you can ask them how they feel about your reaction. It will feel good when s/he says they are happy and enjoyed having time together and thank you for the donuts. You will feel good as s/he leaves the car with a huge smile and a wave. As you complete your drive to work, you can be proud of yourself because you have practiced being self-aware and even asked another for feedback.

In fact, asking for other's feedback about yourself can help you get a 360-degree view of yourself. Putting this information with your own viewpoints can help you evaluate yourself and have a broader picture of your strengths and weakness with respect to self-awareness. It can help you learn where your blind spots are. However, make sure you are asking the right person. Choose someone who has your best interests at heart.

Close examination of yourself in this way can help you assess yourself and can reveal areas where you are confident and areas where you lack it. Doing this can also reveal beliefs that you hold about yourself, both positive and negative. When you have negative feelings about yourself, it can have an impact on how you interact with the world. When people do not love themselves, they create a strange dynamic with how they deal with other people. On one hand, they accept a lot of poor treatment from other people. On the other hand, they also give other people poor treatment because they do not feel like they are a good person.

Self-Assessment tests can also bring to light things about your beliefs and values as well as core characteristics that are key to your personal psyche. It can be helpful and even fun to learn personality types and information they can reveal about you. They should not be used with a grain of salt because your own personal state of mind can come into play. Also, people tend to try to select the most socially acceptable responses, which can skew the test results. Well-respected tests include the following:

- DiSC, which was introduced by Walter Clark in 1940, is generally used in a corporate environment and measures Dominance, Influence, Conscientiousness, and Steadfastness. It reveals the qualities of leadership and the ability to function in a team setting.

- HEXACO, which was developed in 2000 and measures honesty-humility, emotionality, extraversion, agreeableness, conscientiousness, openness to experience.

- Neo Personality Inventory was developed in the 1970s by Costa and McCrae though it was revised in 2005 and measures openness to experience, conscientiousness, extraversion, agreeableness, and neuroticism.

- Myers-Briggs Type Indicator was created by Katharine Cook Briggs and her daughter, Isabel Briggs Myers, in the 1940s. It helps in learning how different personality types relate to the world around them and their varying ways of making decisions.

- Eysenck Personality Inventory focuses on whether a person is introverted or extraverted and where they fall in the spectrum of stability versus neurotic.

While personality tests are not meant to be taken as law, they are a guide to helping you explore yourself. You can figure out where you are, and then that will help you figure out where you want to be and how to get there.

Another point is to be aware of these assumptions you may have about yourself and others. The reason it is healthy to have assumptions about ourselves and know what they are is that when you are aware of the assumptions, you can examine whether or not they are justified and valid. It would be worthwhile to make a list of your own personal beliefs about yourself. These might include "I am a helpful person and a good team player," "I'm a good trainer for new employees," and "I'm not good at talking in front of large groups." The first two assumptions about teamwork and the ability to impart knowledge are very positive. These are things that may actually come up in annual reviews, so they are validated. If the second point about training new employees has not been mentioned in the review; however, it is something you should talk with management about so you can be pulled into onboarding plans for new employees. The third point, however, could be a faulty assumption. It is rare to have a natural public speaking, and it is something that can be developed. Public speaking is learnable, and with some coaching, most people can gain the ability to get through at least a short speech.

There may be things you learn about yourself, which could improve your life. Perhaps you discover, "I am a workaholic." This is both a positive and a negative. It implies dedication to your job and a desire for upward mobility. Employers love workaholics because they tend to really care about their job and their performance. A workaholic places their job very high on their priority list. On the other hand, being aware of one's workaholic tendencies can help a person to keep their work-life balance in mind so that it doesn't take an undue toll on family relationships. The workaholic needs to put limits on himself/herself, which includes phone/laptop timeouts so they can be fully present for family outings and vacations. In addition, mealtime needs to be sacred, and the workaholic cannot "talk shop" or take calls during family mealtime. Workaholics tend to work late a lot, so perhaps one night a week, they should come home on time and have Family Fun Night with plans whether they are staying in, playing games and ordering pizza or a family trip to the zoo or park.

Your own assumptions about others should also be examined. These beliefs can have a direct impact on how we feel and how we behave towards others, which also impacts how we are seen socially. If we are overly suspicious of other people's motivations and feel that other people are "out to get me," it can make us behave negatively around others and actually miss out on possible opportunities and positive relationships with people. Biases about other people because of their culture, race, or religion can make one miss out on a personally enriching friendship and eye-opening experiences. Each culture has some very positive things to offer than will broaden one's horizons. Think of the food alone! A negative attitude makes us present with an ungainly countenance instead of a nice smile. Beyond that, negative assumptions about others also make us behave in a less than friendly way. No one wants to be known as the scowling unfriendly person that we surely will present ourselves to be if we carry negative presumptions about others in our hearts.

On the other hand, as we honestly assess ourselves, this type of trait can be recognized and changed. Remember, what is known can be changed. Sometimes we fear things we do not understand. What if we recognized this fear instead, and approached the other person in the spirit of learning something new? In this way, we can overcome the negative bias that is doing nothing positive for our life and replace that behavior with something warmer. We all understand that someone showing negative emotions are not putting their best foot forward.

The state of being self-aware is such an important component of emotional intelligence that it is worthwhile to do these exercises. Being self-aware acts as a confidence booster and can improve social relationships as an added bonus. In addition, the self-honesty and introspection can soothe areas of our emotional health that need healing. Others will notice the positive change in you and may even ask what has changed. It could open the dialog for deeper learning, and the other person may be interested in embarking on a similar journey. You could say that being self-aware is good for our general well-being. We are happier when we are self-aware because then we do not continuously make mistakes and then wonder what is driving us to act in certain unpleasant ways.

Try this as an exercise, think about two recent social situations, one that was very positive and one where you felt your performance was not as positive as it could have been. Perhaps one could be a task you were given and work, and perhaps one is a family interaction where something unexpected happened, or you needed to give negative feedback. Write down your feelings about each along with any biases you carried into the situation. What was the outcome of each situation? What does it reveal about yourself? Do your findings challenge anything you think about yourself or the others involved? How did your actions impact the relationship? Write down what you might have done differently. Flip that over and think about what you felt went very well. You need to complete this part of the exercise as well because it positively reinforces your behavior. Can you think of any ways that are farther-reaching than the current circumstance in which the positive behaviors have impacted your relationships?

Congratulate yourself! You are now one of the few people who give themselves this level of self-care. When we learn about ourselves and seek to improve ourselves, we are giving to ourselves. When we improve ourselves, we are not selfish. We are actually practicing care for each and every relationship we have in our lives. As we improve how we interact and are seen in society, we increase our standing with the people we care about. We also leave an imprint on others with whom we interact and inspire them to do the same.

You need to be able to admit things to yourself so you can speak your truth. Let's say a friend invites you to go out with them today, but you are feeling tired and do not want to go. Deep inside, you know you do not want to because if you did, you would be getting up and ready to go, but instead, you are dragging your feet and looking at the clock with dread until it is time to go. You might think it is the kind thing to do to deny your true feelings and go out with them, all the while suffering, but this is not so. For one, you will not be feeling well and looking at the clock to see how long before this is over, so you will not be enjoying yourself. Your friend will not be having a good time either. People can tell when they are out with someone who does not want to be there, and it is an uncomfortable feeling. There really is no such thing as suffering in silence. It shows in your facial expressions. They will hear the tone in your voice and know you are not enthusiastic about this. They will then feel guilty about dragging you along.

This is why you need to be honest and tell your friend you are not feeling well and ask to reschedule. You may feel like you are letting them down, but it is actually a mature thing to do. It is a part of growing up. You are going to have to disappoint people sometimes. You will have to tell them things that are not pleasing to them. Self-awareness means having to let go of the desire to make everyone else happy and for them to perceive you as a good person. People will sometimes tell one another upsetting news. As a child, you think, "I will do this because it is what people want me to do." You go to your bedroom based on a bedtime that was set up for you, and if you are still awake, you conceal it so as not to make someone upset. You follow the rules and curfews to stay out of trouble. However, as a person becomes an adult, they learn to make their own decisions. They start to find their own identity. Let's go back to the friend who asked you to hang out. If you are honest with them and tell them you don't feel up to it today, you could reschedule for a day where you actually feel like it, and the two of you will have a much better time for it.

You might think you are letting people down when you speak your truth, but actually, they will respect you more for it. People do not have respect for people; they do not feel like they can get the truth out of. If you are trying to do get through something because someone else wanted to do it, they will notice it. From your point of view, you are a good friend because you are trying to hold up to what you said you were going to do, but from their point of view, they have realized it is within you to lie to them. Even if it is supposed to be a benevolent one, it is still a lie. You are still disingenuous.

It is difficult to find an identity if you grew up in a situation where you needed to be things for other people all the time. However, as an adult, those people do not have your livelihood in their hands. Definitely, do not let a version of them you have conjured up limit you in what you can do. If they are no longer in your life, they do not get a say in what you do.

Accepting yourself as an imperfect person will actually make you much happier. If you hold yourself to a standard of being perfect, you will be devastated when you do not live up to this standard. As humans, we make mistakes every day, even if they are little ones. This means you will constantly be disappointed in yourself.

Self-acceptance is a part of self-awareness. Everyone comes with their own set of strengths and weaknesses. If you think someone you know is perfect, it means you don't spend a great deal of time with them. Everyone has things about them that make them hard to deal with at times.

If you have had negative experiences in your life, you need to acknowledge and deal with them. If you do not, they will come out in ways you did not expect or want, and they could end up hurting various aspects of your life.

Think about a person who had parents who were unkind to them with their words. They never missed an opportunity to point out a mistake they made or to make an ugly remark to them. Let's say this person did not acknowledge what they went through and kept this bottled up, thinking they wouldn't have to think about it again after they moved out of their parent's house. However, as they navigate through life, they find it hard to maintain friendships and relationships, and that they often end chaotically. They have frequent disagreements with other people, and they don't understand why they are personally attacked so much more than everyone else.

They are not really being accosted any more or less than anyone else. The problem lies in their perception of what other people do. They do not realize they are still carrying their poor treatment by their parents with them, and so they see it in other people, even when they might not have actually done anything wrong. This means they take things as insults that might not have been intended that way. Someone might say a sentence to them that their parents would say before insulting them. It might be a very innocuous-sounding one, and that is why the other person is left so confused when their friend gets angry at them. They do not know this person's history, so the only thing they can see of the situation is that they made a casual, offhand comment and then had their head bitten off over it. People naturally respond to a confrontational attitude with defensiveness, which confirms their beliefs. Only when this person comes to realize their upbringing affected them in negative ways can they begin to move toward different behavior.

The first step to getting better is to understand why the problem is there. As a disclaimer, this is not the same as excusing the behavior. If someone consistently treats you badly and then follows it up with tragic stories, they are not good to you, and you need to get out of this situation unless and until they can learn to better handle their emotion. If this is something you find yourself consistently doing, it is time to take steps to change this behavior. True self-awareness is not letting yourself off easy because you have been through a hard time and explaining away bad behavior with it. It is learning where the bad behavior comes from and taking steps to correct it.

Be sure that what you are feeling is accurate instead of using emotional reasoning. Basically, this means when we judge reality based on feelings and thoughts- "It must be true if I think it is." Many times, we use emotional reasoning in reference to other people; for example, "My friend must be angry at me because I have a feeling they are." Did you know you can also use emotional reasoning to make incorrect assumptions about your own feelings and thoughts?

Here's how it works. You wake up late because you slept through your alarm, leaving you barely enough time to get ready for work, which leaves you walking in the building a few minutes late. Your boss chides you for this and tells you that you need to pick up the pace of your work. This leaves you feeling stressed, nervous, and irritated. Your coworker makes an unkind comment about your outfit, which makes you feel self-conscious. You feel like the world is out to get you today.

You go home and watch your favorite show, and when something upsetting happens on it, you have an extremely emotional reaction to it, crying too excessively for what is a typical reaction to a TV show. You might think you are responding to the scene, but you are actually crying about the day you had. It is the "straw that broke the camel's back." Seeing something upsetting conjured up all of the emotions you had experienced throughout the day. Yet you might think to yourself, "It must be about the TV show. I didn't cry over anything that happened today as it was happening. It was only when I was watching this show. Maybe I shouldn't watch it anymore if it makes me become this upset." This means you are unnecessarily giving up something you love.

This is how emotional reasoning can be harmful to our lives and relationships. Sometimes we take anger out on the people we love that is really directed at another source. In the moment and even long after, we can become convinced our anger really was at this person, even if it wasn't.

At the end of the day, sort through your emotions. See if there is something you need to address. Sometimes we can be stressed out or upset about something and not even realize it, and that is when it is the most damaging to us. For instance, you realize your partner has been neglecting to put a coaster under their drink, and it has become a consistent thing. It is good to come to the realization that this is upsetting you because then you can have a productive conversation with them about it later where the end result is the problem being solved as opposed to having a sudden and incendiary argument with them.

If you have felt a change in your emotional pattern lately, you need to take note of this. If you become angry or cry more easily lately, you need to be sure to understand where that is coming from. Maybe you are worried about someone or have gotten some bad news recently, and therefore you are feeling emotionally fragile right now. When you realize something is bothering you, you will be a step closer to being in control of your reaction to the negative emotion.

CHAPTER 3:
SELF-REGULATION

A person who is self-aware can also regulate their own responses in social situations. This helps them control their reactions and remain in control. The person who remains calm finds it easier to get what they want in a situation and keep things from going negative.

Everyone has gotten bad news at a time when they were not able to react right away. Perhaps a repair is going to cost more than you thought, and your children are sitting right there. You don't want to frighten them, so you take a deep breath and answer the repairman to continue with fixing the problem, and your mind goes forward on how you can adjust your spending, knowing that you will have a little extra on your credit card. You just practiced self-regulation. It's possible you felt angry and upset. Some people tend to want to cry when they are upset while others become angry. Whichever the case may be, it's important to be able to recognize those feelings and use some calming techniques. It's healthy to have the reactions and emotions, but it is equally as important to be able to remain calm. You may even need to put off your natural reaction to a time that is more appropriate.

Most of us who have ever been in a relationship have experienced relationship trouble. Perhaps you have been in an argument about something and had a bad night.

Tomorrow at work, you feel over-tired and crabby. You might even receive a cantankerous text from your partner, and it fuels your anger. Truly it is ill-advised to discuss the argument with your coworkers because that just damages your character in their eyes. Taking your frustration out on your coworkers is also not an option because you could damage your working relationships, which need to be strong. One approach might be texting your partner back that you want to end the argument and make up. Tell them you cannot continue the discussion while you are at work. Stress can make us breathe shallow and not enough, so inhale slowly pause at the top of the breath for just a pulse and let the breath out slowly. Repeat this a couple of times. You may also want to get a cup of tea. Chamomile, peppermint, or green tea are excellent options that are known to help with stress and can bring a feeling of well-being. Now you have probably self-soothed enough that you can finish your day.

The point is to lessen the intensity of the emotion in times where it would be inappropriate to express strong emotion. The waitress who keeps a smile on her face even though a customer is rude and irrational is expressing self-regulation. She does not want to call attention to the situation, and she wants to keep the patron from becoming more upset and louder. She knows that if she does her best to make the dining experience pleasant that the customer will eventually leave.

Similarly, the teacher who gets a visit from an upset student about a grade they received needs to practice self-regulation. Remaining calm is very important, as is firmly sticking to the procedure. If it's appropriate, the teacher may choose to offer some extra credit. If that is not possible, the teacher can advise that the student attends group study meetings so they can improve their overall score for the class. In this instance, s/he also has an opportunity to both demonstrate and instruct the student on self-regulation. By keeping his/her own emotions minimized, the teacher can help the student recognize their own emotions. Perhaps the teacher can give the student some tips to lessen their reaction to the bad grade. Also, by helping him/her to plan on how to improve their overall score in the class, s/he is giving the student lifelong skills they can use when emotions feel overwhelming.

Self-regulation is an integral part of emotional intelligence because it helps us to cauterize explosive behavior in others as well as helping us to keep our own emotions in check. Both of these things increase our feeling of well-being and improve health. By practicing self-regulation, we strengthen our relationships and improve our self-image and reputation.

Even the most emotionally intelligent person has base impulses. "That person cut me off on the road, I want to make an obscene hand gesture at them." "My partner came home late last night; they must be having an affair! I'm going to get the truth out of them right now." "My child knocked something over that is important to me; I want to scream at them." If you have impulses and images that flash through your mind of saying or doing things that are unkind, you are not alone. Everyone has them from time to time. In fact, everyone has them from day-to-day. Think of the kindest person you have ever met. It might be the lady who runs the donut shop or your grandfather. Even they have unkind thoughts from time to time. However, they do not act on them, and then they let them pass. This is because they practice self-regulation.

Self-regulation is an often-misunderstood aspect of emotional intelligence. It is sometimes interpreted as keeping your emotions inside. This is actually the opposite of self-regulation because if you bottle all of your emotions inside you will end up expressing them in a very unhealthy way. This concept is not at all about not allowing yourself to express your emotions. It is about finding the right way to go about expressing them.

Sometimes we deny our thoughts and make them even stronger by repressing them. We think the thought we are having makes us bad people, and so we condemn ourselves for it. This is not necessary. Often, by the time you realize you have a grievance about someone, it has been going on for a while. The first thought you have about it will not be a pleasant one. It is not to be taken seriously, either. It is simply your brain trying to get your attention. It tells you something extreme to get your attention so it can then let you know there is a problem.

For example, you have a friend who is in an on-again, off-again relationship. They are either upset because the relationship is coming to an end again or because they are together, and it is not going well. Either way, you need to be a source of emotional support for them on a consistent basis, and you are tired of hearing about the same problem. The first thought that goes through your head might be something harsh, like "They're so annoying, I never want to talk to them again!" You might be horrified at yourself for thinking that, but this is what it really means, which is why you should not take it at face value. After you analyze this thought for a while, you come to realize you are not annoyed with them, and you do not want to cut the ties with them forever. You are annoyed with something they are doing, and you do not want to talk about their relationship anymore.

Your negative emotions are the ones you need to express the most. The other person may not even know they have done something to offend you, so nothing is going to change until you bring it up. They cannot read your mind. Wishing they would see that something they do bothers you will only lead to you feeling more and more resentful of them. Trying to drop subtle cues that you want them to pick up on is a mind game. You need to tell them straight out. However, this will need to be done with tact so you will get your desired results instead of damaging the relationship.

You must tell others what you are feeling in a way that is palatable. This has a lot to do with how you word your grievances. If it feels accusatory, the other person is naturally going to become defensive, so you will not get the response you wanted and, therefore, will not feel heard. No one will respond well when they feel like they are being attacked.

In order to prevent this, avoid saying things like "you always talk over me" or "you never listen to me." This is a hurtful thing to say, and it is not true. There is almost nothing that always or never happens. You are trying to share a grievance about something that is done sometimes by a person you overall like and care about, so you need to make sure you convey this message. Instead, try saying, "It hurts me when you interrupt me because I don't feel like you want to hear what I have to say."

Let's think about the friend who talks about their on-again, off-again relationship too much. You are going to need to be direct with what you say, and so, therefore, it might sound a little blunt to them. However, if you present your plight to them in a way that does not try to tear at their dignity or insult them, you might be able to find a way to fix the problem. Say something like, "I want to spend time with you, but I think we need to set some ground rules. We can talk about each other's problems, but it can't take up all of our time together." Sometimes, even if it is more their habit than yours, it is helpful to say, "we need to work on something." This way, it feels less like they are being called to the carpet and will be more able to listen. If you present your problem this way, you might be able to come up with a solution. You can talk about personal problems for a set time, but then it has to come to a close. On the other hand, if you come at them with accusations and anger, you might lose the friendship.

If they are unwilling to work towards a better relationship, you can then make your decision about whether or not you want to keep them as a friendship. However, if you tell them what is bothering you, there is the opportunity for mending fences. The ball will be in their court then.

Self-regulation does not mean you will never have thoughts that are disrespectful. It means they will not come out of your mouth. It means you are going to wait a minute before you react so that you do not respond to transient feelings in a way that will affect your life long-term. Transient feelings are ones that are temporary. They are fleeting bits of strong emotion, also known as a moment of passion. You might be having a heated argument with a dear friend and think, "I hate them!" This is not how you really feel. You are having that thought because you are intensely angry with them at this moment. That is why it is called a transient feeling because it is only going to be here for a long time. That is why it is important not to speak during this time because you might say something you will regret later.

You also do not want to act based on positive transient feelings. An example of this is when people get into a very serious relationship too quickly. They are having feelings of infatuation for this person, so of course, they feel like they are going to stay in love with this person. However, if you have only been with a person for a few months, you do not truly know them. You only know them when they are dressed up and on their best behavior. You have never been in a serious argument with them. You have never had the shared responsibility of paying bills. You do not know their more unpleasant habits, and everyone has them.

One of the ways to prevent doing or saying things you will regret later is to just count to ten. Just pause for a moment before speaking. What you are feeling might not be accurate and merely a product of temporary anger. If you tell your friend something harsh, they will remember it permanently, and then they will wonder if that is what you really think of them.

If you are exchanging messages with someone and things are starting to get heated, now is the time to step away from your phone for a little while and distract yourself. Nothing else productive will come of the conversation right now. You will only hurt each other. It is easier to say hurtful things to people over a keyboard because you are not looking at them. Not being face-to-face with them also gives a sense of security. It can make you forget that you are talking to a person you care about and not just a text message. This feeling of security can lead to arguments getting more out of hand at a faster rate. When you are starting to realize that the conversation has stopped being productive and started to become a trading of insults and zings, it is time to put the phone down for a little while.

You should never let yourself be a doormat. However, if you are going to preserve your relationships, you need to pick your battles, which means there are certain things you will need to let go of. If something is an isolated incident and it doesn't happen again in the future, it is probably not something you need to talk about.

On the flip side of this, you need to know when to speak up. It is actually practicing self-regulation to address a grievance you have about something someone else is doing. For example, you feel like your roommate could contribute more to the upkeep of the house. It is not fair to you to bear the full responsibility of cleaning, so it is your right and responsibility to bring it up to them before it comes out in a rush. However, remember this. Even if you have a legitimate gripe about someone, there is a way to go about letting them know of it. You just want this behavior to stop, not to hurt them. Nothing good comes of putting things unnecessarily harshly.

You might get a moment of satisfaction from saying something harsh. You might feel like you got back and them and were able to say your piece, but you will not feel that way later. When it has damaged your relationship, you will regret it and need to apologize. We all need to give an apology sometimes, but you can take steps to make it so that those moments do not happen as often. In the case of the roommate who needs to put in more effort, try saying something like, "I think we should divide the household chores so that one person does not wind up feeling overworked." This way, you have spoken your mind without being unnecessarily hurtful. If you had said something like "Clean this place up! It looks like a mess unless I do something about it!", this will only hurt their feelings. They will not be as willing to listen to your plight even though it is valid, because you have gone on the attack.

Physical activity will also help you with self-regulation. Sometimes when you are angry, it helps you to let it out physically. This does not mean break something or hit a wall, which is destroying property and putting yourself at risk of getting injured. If you feel like it needs to be a damage-causing activity, take up kickboxing. You can also go for a run or do some other form of workout. Even going outside for a walk can help.

Self-regulation also means to move on at some point. When something happens that is upsetting to you, it is devastating, even if it is not the most major thing that could happen. You are entitled to your pain, but you also need to move on from it at some point. If you do not, you will be stuck in that same place, wishing things could be different but knowing they cannot be. This will cause those same feelings to keep coming up, and you will go into that same dark place.

For example, if you lose a friendship, it is understandable to grieve for that loss. However, you cannot let yourself be controlled by this pain. Otherwise, you will go to places that will special to you and your friend and experience the same spells of anger and sorrow. You will not get to the point where you are not crying anymore about it, which is an extremely unhealthy thing. Staying in a place of sorrow will get nothing accomplished. When your emotions are running high for a prolonged period of time, you are at risk for having more breakdowns. You can suffer physically.

This is why self-regulation is dependent upon leaving the past behind. Making yourself miserable over the things you have done wrong in the past will not make it so that you can go back in time and undo your mistakes. Wishing something bad had not happened to you will not erase it. Feeling like there was something someone who should have done something for you, but they didn't will only fill you with negative emotions.

If there is someone you are holding a grudge against, it is extremely important that you let it go. Some people find it useful to do something symbolic when they are trying to get over something from the past. In order to get over bad feelings towards someone, a popular method is to write their name on a piece of paper. If you want to write what you resent them for on that paper, you are free to do so. Then, in a safe method, you burn the piece of paper. The idea is that when the paper dissipates, so does the negativity. They are no longer a part of your life. Then you must forgive the person so you can move on with your life.

Forgiveness is not about letting someone off easy or forgetting that they hurt or lied to you. It is actually about freeing yourself. Think about it. When you carry a grudge against someone, it takes up a lot of your time. There is seething involved. This means you miss out on opportunities to feel happy. Your anger against this person has probably ruined entire days for you that could have been fun. While you are stuck living in a time where they hurt you, where are they? They are probably off living their life, having fun, doing whatever they want to do. It is very unlikely that they are thinking about you. You being angry at them has not caused any impedance in their life, only yours. It also hurts one's spirit to hold a grudge. You have to have negative feelings towards them. This also means you are likely holding ill will towards them and wishing some form of a bad thing to happen to them. When you send an ill wish toward someone else, it only damages your life because you are sending out negative energy. At that point, who is really the person in the wrong?

When you forgive someone, they will never be a part of your life again. You are now free to do what you want and move on to your next chapter. It is actually much more of a favor to yourself than it is a favor to them.

It is difficult not to take something someone else says or does personally whenever it causes you pain, but you need to for the sake of your own sanity. Even if a person claims they did something because of you, it was still about them. For example, you bump into someone in a crowded hallway, and the person says something rude to you. Even though their words are directed at you, it is still because of a flaw within them and not because of what you did. Most of the time, when people bump into one another, there is a mutual apology to one another, and then both people move on. It is unlikely that either person will remember the event the next day. If someone gets angry over something like that, it is because they have a problem controlling their anger. If they cannot control themselves any better than that, they need to take a look at themselves. You do not need to chide yourself over it. What we do is our choice. Even if another person causes us to feel an emotion, it is still our choice when we react irrationally.

We are all human, which means there will be times that you have an improper response to something. You might have had a long, stressful day, and then you get irrationally angry at someone for something minor. Recognizing when you have done something wrong is a part of self-regulation because it keeps history from repeating itself. While it may be tempting to think, "I had a right to react that way to them after the kind of day I had," this is an unhealthy way to think. Being stressed out is not a reason to be rude to other people.

It is much more difficult to self-regulate if you do not give yourself time to relax. In the evening, start to create a ritual for winding down. It will help you sleep better, and it will also help you to have some time where your mind is not racing. There comes a point in the evening where it is time to put away responsibilities. This is why it is advisable to complete any tasks you need to before the sun goes down. This way, there can come a point where you shut the day away. Make your bedroom more than just where you go to recharge before you start the day. Make it a place you enjoy being in and consider to be a safe haven. Before you sleep, you might enjoy listening to new age instrumental music and closing your eyes. Music has a strong influence on our minds, and when you play calming music, it can help to lower your stress levels. Lighting a candle can have a similar effect. It helps build a good atmosphere and makes your room smell pleasant.

Stress management is a large part of self-regulation. When you feel like you could blow at any second, you are going to have a hard time controlling your emotions. They will feel overwhelming. Yoga and meditation are go-to's for many people in the way of stress relief, but you also need to find what works for you. As long as it is not self-destructive and it helps you not to feel as upset and anxious, it is a good idea. Feeling happy, even for just a moment, can break the cycle of feeling stressed out for a little while and end up making the levels of anxiety lower because they haven't had so much time to fester, and they also haven't gotten to do it on a constant basis.

You will also benefit from working on your social circle. Spending time with friends is a good way to relieve stress. For one, you can tell your friends about your problems. They might know a way to help you find a solution for them, and if not, at the very least, you can vent to them. Our problems often feel smaller just by saying them out loud to someone because it makes you feel like you are not alone. Also, when you spend time with people, it helps you not to think as much about the things that are causing you distress. They serve as a distraction for a little while, and they also make the stressful situation not seem like as big of a deal. If you just go to and from work, a problem at work will feel like your whole world. When you have people to spend time with during evenings and weekends, you can get a break from that. This is why it is so important to cultivate a social life.

Chapter 4:
Social Skills

When in social situations, one needs to know his own position in relation to others. A person who is socially aware generally listens closely and pays attention to non-verbal communication. This is a key component of developing leadership skills.

Social skills are basically the way we interact with people. You use them every day in every situation, even if you are just on the phone ordering a pizza. You have to communicate to them what you want and where you live. You are giving them information in a way that is they can receive it.

You might have the idea that has been cultivated through TV and movies that people are liked based on what they wear or whether or not they can accomplish the ever-elusive concept that is being "cool." However, this is not entirely accurate. Social skills have much more to do with treating people in a way that makes them feel like they are valued. People like people who treat them well.

When you are out with people, you need to appear sure of yourself. This is why it is better to just be yourself. If you try to display an image of yourself that is not you, your insecurity will show through, which will not help you socially. When someone is insecure, it makes other people uncomfortable because then they feel like they cannot be themselves around you.

There is a difference between "doing as the Romans do when you are in Rome," or going along with the customs of the house you are in and trying to put on a false image of yourself. It is perfectly fine to go along with the tradition if you are visiting a family who says grace before every meal. In fact, it is a show of respect. However, you should not make yourself out to have an identity that you do not. For example, do not dress in a style you do not like and present yourself as a person who regularly dresses this way. People can sense when you are not genuine, and you will be considered a chameleon, which is not a good thing. If you do not appear to have an authentic self, people will have a hard time trusting that what you say is true. This makes you come off as untrustworthy. They might even think you have some sort of unknown agenda.

Presenting yourself as a different person to get people to like you is a form of manipulation. This is because they are not being given the full story. Instead, they are being dealt with underhanded tactics. This means they are making decisions without having knowledge that might make them change their minds. When your deceit is found out, the people you were trying to impress will not appreciate it.

The person who is truly "cool" is the person who can embrace their own identity. If you do this, your life will be much easier. This way, you will not have to go through that uncomfortable moment where you have to reveal your real self to the person after having deceived them for a long time.

When you meet a new person, ask them about themselves. If they bring up a movie they like, ask them what it is about and who is in it. They will appreciate this because people like it when they feel like someone is taking an interest in the things they like.

You do not need to change anything about the core of your personality to have social skills. However, there are habits you can acquire to make yourself seem more sociable. That is actually one of the first steps to having social skills. You need to present yourself to the world as a person who wants to be social. This means you need to have an open face and body language. For example, crossing your arms is a body language sign that says to other people, "leave me alone." This is because it is a metaphorical way of closing you off from the world. You place a barrier between you and other people. In the movies, when someone is closed off, there is a person that comes along who is determined to break through their barriers and become a friend to them. In real life, people will see that they are somewhere they are not wanted, and they will leave.

Social skills are about little acts of kindness. When someone is carrying something heavy, open the door for them. If they drop something and it has landed near you, pick it up for them. These little things can actually mean more than a grand gesture would. Coming across as a kind and considerate person will make people like you. As you come into adolescence, you might think you need to act like you do not care about anything in order to appear "cool." This is not true. The only people who really do this are people who are unsure of themselves.

You might be tempted to pretend to like things other people do and not talk about things they don't. However, people might actually like you more if you do talk about what you actually like. People who are passionate about something come off as more interesting than people who go along with everything. This is especially important if you are on a date with someone. Smiling, nodding, and agreeing with everything they say will actually be a turnoff for them. People do not like it when they are with someone who will not contribute to the conversation. You also run the risk of giving off the impression that you are uncomfortable if you do not say anything.

It is important to learn a person's name when you meet them. It means more to people than you might think if you learn their name. It makes them feel like you remember them, and therefore they feel like they are significant to you. People have a natural liking for people who consider them to be important. This is why you should repeat a person's name when they say it to you. This way, you will be certain of what their name is, and the repetition will help you commit it to memory. Say it a few more times during the conversation. People like to hear their name being spoken. When your conversation with them is coming to an end, say their name one more time as you are saying goodbye to them. This way, their name will still be fresh on your mind when the conversation is over.

When you first meet someone, ask them questions about themselves, and commit their answers to memory. It means a lot to people when you remember the things they say. It lets them know they are being listened to. It is a basic emotional need to feel like you are being heard. Along with listening, talk to them about yourself too. While over-sharing is something to avoid, you also should give bits of information about yourself while meeting someone. If they don't know anything about you, it is harder to make a connection. People feel suspicion about someone who keeps their cards too close to the vest. Share things that happened to you today with the person you are speaking to and listen to stories of theirs. When people swap stories about their personal life with one another, they feel more comfortable with one another. You feel like you know one another better, and when someone tells you about an experience, they have had, in a way you share it with them. You may not have been there, but you visualize it and picture how that situation must have made them feel. When you have that type of connection with a person, you become closer to them.

Commit the things they tell you to memory and ask about them the next time you see the person. For example, if they tell you they're going to have a job interview soon, ask them how it went the next time you see them. This will let the person know you were listening to them.

Notice a pattern in these bits of advice. None of them encourages you to change anything about your own personality. You became the person you are now because of the walk of life you come from. Your own personal experiences have shaped your unique perspective about life. The person you are now is valuable, and there are people who would be honored to have your friendship. You may admire the personalities of other people, but that is their own unique one that has been cultivated over the course of their life. If you were to try to imitate theirs, it would come off as forced, and it would not be sustainable. You cannot take someone else's personality on as your own, but you can learn how to use the one you have to become the best friend and leader.

Having social skills is a very important part of leadership. You can have great ideas and high levels of intelligence, but if you cannot present these ideas to people in a way that it sounds appealing to them, all of your talents cannot be put to use.

This is why there tend to be two minds behind an organization, one being the "brains" of the operation who comes up with the great plans, while the other is the one who communicates these plans to their people. Both people are valuable to the organization, but the fact remains that you can only go so far without being able to influence people.

As a disclaimer, influencing is not the same as manipulating people. The biggest difference between the two is what place they are coming from when a person does it. A person who is being manipulative has something they want from you, but they will not tell you what their intentions are, so they use underhanded tactics to get it. Through covert means, they want to force you to do what they want. For example, "If you really loved me, you would buy that for me." This is something a child would do to lead their parents to buy them a toy as opposed to just asking them for it and accepting the prospect of the answer being no.

Influencing is also something a person does when they are trying to convince someone else to take a certain course of action, which is why people get the two of them confused. They come at it from an honest place and let the other person know what their intentions are. They tell them what decision they think they should make and why, and if the other person still does not wish to do this, they let it go. An example of this would be a friend telling another friend that they do not advise they date a particular person because they have a history of cheating on their partners. They might say something like, "I know you like him, but I've met three of his past girlfriends, and all of them told me he was unfaithful to them. I just don't want to see you get hurt." In this scenario, the friend is not holding anything back. She has a message she wants to convey, and she conveys it clearly.

That ties into another part of social skills. You need to make your intentions and messages clear. It is comforting for people when they feel like they know what you want. If you want a favor from someone, just ask them for it. Manipulation might be tempting because it doesn't give them the opportunity to refuse you, but it actually winds up damaging your relationships because people do not like it. On the other hand, they will respect you more if they find out they can tell you know and you will take it well, and that they will still have your friendship. If you need to vent to someone, you need to tell them straight up what is going on. Do not make them drag it out of you. This is frustrating, as well as concerning.

In order to have social skills, you have to remember to remain positive. Think about the most popular people in your school or work environment. They probably greet people in the morning with a smile and have an upbeat attitude. They want to bring other people's moods up. This is attractive to people. They want to be near people who are positive because just as bad moods are contagious, so are good ones.

If you have a negative attitude, this is going to drive people away. It also puts you at risk for creating a self-fulfilling prophecy. For example, Carrie is unhappy with her life right now because her social circle is not what she wants it to be.

She has difficulty making and keeping friends. She believes it is because people do not think she is "cool" and therefore leave her out on sight. However, there are other habits she has that play a much bigger role in the outcome of her social interactions than she realizes. When she goes out, she looks at the people around her with envy because they have friends, and she does not. This leads to her feeling resentment for them. As humans, what we feel shows on our faces. Even if we do not express something vocally, our body language and facial expressions give it away.

For Carrie, the jealousy and resentment she feels in the inside show on the outside, as her arms are crossed and her face is set in a glaring expression. This is not going to make people want to approach you. In fact, they might think you are looking at them with a scowl because you do not like them. This means they think you want them to leave you alone, and therefore they will. Carrie also expresses her negative attitudes verbally. When she is around people, she expresses her cynical attitudes about life and people, and how she thinks they are generally bad. She also talks about how she feels cheated out of a lot of things. She thinks other people just get friends and opportunities, and she doesn't, and that there is no reason behind this. Her bitter disposition makes the people around her feel uncomfortable because when someone has a negative attitude, they cause the aura in the room to be heavy. When one person in the room is in a bad mood, it tends to spread around to everyone else.

Carrie carries a lot of jealousy towards her coworker, Vicki, because she is well-liked by her co-workers. This feeling escalates when she learns that Vicki has gotten a promotion. She thinks there is a force in the universe that dislikes her and prefers Vicki, and that's why she gets all the breaks that she doesn't. The real reason Vicki has an ampler social life and is more successful is that she has social skills. She comes to work every day with a smile on her face, and she greets everyone as she walks by, asking them how they are doing. When something needs to be done, she is the first to volunteer. When someone doesn't understand what is going on, she goes out of her way to help them, whereas Carrie gets annoyed. Vicki also leaves her personal problems at the door while Carrie tells her coworkers about them in great detail, causing discomfort for them.

Carrie is reactive. She doesn't take an active role in her own life. She lets life happen around her and then becomes upset when things do not go as she wants them to. She complains about being dissatisfied with her life but never does anything to try to change her circumstances. She puts out negative energy, and therefore the people in her life are also negative, and then their relationship is chaotic.

Vicki is proactive. She knows what she wants, and she goes after it. She has a positive outlook on life and therefore thinks she has the power to influence what happens in her life. She is a positive person, and therefore she seeks out positive people, and they gravitate towards her to build a healthy relationship.

There are certain things in life we cannot control. However, we are not helpless. Our destiny is not laid out for us in a way that we cannot influence it. When a situation is thrown at us, we can decide how we react to it. For example, when a person says something rude to you, you have a choice in how their behavior is going to affect you. You can hold onto it, letting it ruin your day and cause you to become irritable, and therefore passing on the negativity to other people. You can also decide you are not going to think about one person saying something rude and moving on with your day, possibly ending on a much better note than what you started with. Taking personal responsibility may seem like a daunting task, but it is actually a liberating one. When you began to claim ownership over your own actions, you can choose how your day goes. You are not at the mercy of outside forces who might not be concerned about your happiness. You are the one in the driver's seat, and therefore you can have a good day even if you have suffered some major disappointments.

If you have behaved like Carrie in the past, that does not mean you cannot become like Vicki. It all starts with the simple belief that your life can improve and that you can be the force that makes that happen. That is the first thing you can change: your attitude. Just saying, "I have faith in myself and in others" will be a step in the right direction.

Earlier, we discussed how there will be times that people do not use emotional intelligence in their dealings with us, but that does not mean we can abandon our own emotional intelligence. This does not mean you need to allow yourself to be walked on. It does not mean you need to go out of your way to be friendly to someone after they have been rude to someone. It means you are not going to engage in what they are trying to pull you into.

For example, when someone behaves in an overly confrontational way and says things to you that are meant to anger you and therefore start a conflict with you, this is emotional manipulation. They are saying things they know are inflammatory, often pushing what they know are personal buttons for you, like insulting you about things that are insecurities for you or bringing up things you did in the past that are embarrassing for you to think about. A person like that is just trying to get a rise out of other people, and if they find out they can get one out of you, they will latch onto you. They are waiting for you to snap and when you do, they will then turn the tables on you to claim victimhood, telling others you are the one who is rude to them. Sometimes when the person has particularly insidious intentions, they will use your reactions to try to paint you as emotionally unstable.

This is why you cannot engage with this person. It will be hard to do because everything this person is saying to you is an attempt to start a confrontation with you. For this kind of person, you need to learn to stop absorbing the things they say. This means you must tune them out the same way you would any other obnoxious noise. If you take what they are saying personally, you will suffer. You are not the only person they act this way with. In fact, they probably do not know any other way to interact with people. Make yourself uninteresting to this person. Do not give an emotional reply to them and keep the conversation topic to the task at hand. If they try to bait you with insults and hurtful comments, the best thing you can do is to pretend you did not hear them say anything at all.

Many times, people deal with this type of problem when they are dealing with a difficult ex while trying to manage to co-parent with them. Do not get sucked into it when they try to bring up old fights; call out mistakes you made or put you down about the quality of a partner you were. When they try to say things like this, do not reply to it. Just tell them "it's your turn to have the kids this weekend" or whatever it is that they need to know. This will make them realize they cannot make you get into an emotional confrontation with them. A person who feeds off of conflict will not stay in a place where they are not getting any results for too long. If you are not giving them what they want, they will eventually move on to someone who will.

When we feel the urge to expand our social circles, we can fall into the trap of limiting our own opportunities. You might think there is no opportunity to meet other people. Try thinking of it this way. Everywhere you go, and everyone you see brings an opportunity to meet someone that can become a friend or romantic partner. Part of having social skills is being open to social interaction. If you feel closed off, people will receive this message and, therefore, not approach you. Do not put too many expectations on the first interaction with someone. Just say hello to them and see where it goes from there. Compliment a piece of their outfit. Ask them a question.

There are many things you can use as a conversation starter. Where you are positioned in a building will also have an effect on your prospects for social interactions. If you are near the corner of the room or close to the wall, it will be less likely for you to talk to people because you are away from the crowd.

When you strike up a conversation with a new person, do not be afraid to ask to switch numbers or invite them to get coffee or some other get-together. The worst that can happen is that they say no, and it is unlikely that is going to happen. You might become best friends or only say hello once in a while. Either way, you have spent some time with another person, which begets you meeting another person after that.

Chapter 5:
Empathy

Empathy is the ability to visualize and understand how another person feels. It is very important in social interactions and can help deepen relationships with others and relate to them on a personal level. Many times, people think of empathy as knowing exactly what other people are going through. This is not entirely true. If we have never had personal experience with a particular situation, it is impossible to really understand it and all of the implications that come with it.

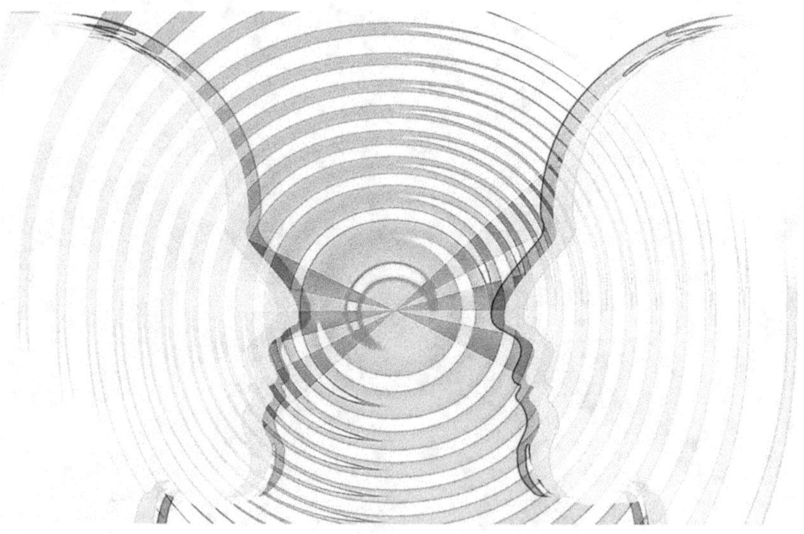

Empathy is actually being able to feel for someone; even you do not understand where they are coming from. It is easy to practice empathy when we agree with a person. You are really put to the test when the person has a belief or standpoint that is different from your own. You do not have to be able to put yourself in a person's shoes to care about them, and everyone has been through something painful. Just tap back into a time that was hard for you to go through, and you can develop an understanding of what is happening to them.

Empathy does not mean you have to change your own opinion. It means you have to uphold respect for another person even though theirs is not the same as yours. Think about how a successful political debate works. The participants do not attack each other's character. It is powerful to say, "I understand what you are trying to say." This is because then the other person feels like you have really heard them. More than for you to agree with them, people want to know they have been heard. This means you think their opinion is valid.

Empathy is especially important in today's society. Right now, we are going through a time of having a very polarized society. Our nation is divided into its mindset. We are on either one side of the political spectrum or the other, and on each side, emotions are running high.

One of the most effective ways to have empathy for people, you do not agree with is to understand that for every topic of debate, both sides make some good points. There is almost no issue that is one-sided. If it was, there would not be such a division among us about it. To take a side on an issue means there are some parts you do not entirely agree with.

For example, let's say you are having a disagreement with your roommate about whether to paint the room blue or yellow. You want it blue, and they want it yellow. Your argument is that blue promotes tranquility and helps to channel intellectual strength, and you worry about the influence of yellow making it hard to relax. Their argument is that yellow is an innately cheerful color and would serve as a mood booster while they are worried about blue because of its connotations of sadness, and they don't want to create that kind of mood in the room. Which one of you is right and who is wrong? The answer is both and neither. Both of you have good ideas about how to structure this room, and there are also cons to both ideas.

You could argue about it until one person gives in and lets the other person have their way. You might give in trying to be a good person, but over time you will look at that yellow room and feel like it was something you had to agree to. If it is them who let you have it painted blue, you might win, but then they will feel slighted, so in a way, you don't really win. However, there is another solution where both of you will have to give something up, but both of you will also benefit.

Say as a compromise you chose to paint the room green, which is what you get when you mix blue and yellow. The color has benefits of both colors while the downsides are mitigated. Green has its own negative connotations, but there is no such thing as a perfect solution. Both of you will look at the color and see traces of your preferred one and know the other did take into consideration what you wanted.

You can miss out on meeting some interesting people and developing some great friendships if you make assumptions about people without taking the time to understand them. People are more than labels. This is especially difficult to deal with in high school, a time where people are especially divided. People are divided off into their own separate cliques, and they do not know much about each other.

Empathy strengthens our friendships. It makes you see beyond the obvious. You know your friends. There are some that you know will break commitments and that you can't trust everything they say, so therefore you need to hold them at arm's length. There are also those who you know are pretty selfish and if you need to talk about yourself, you aren't going to get that from them.

There are others who are more dependable than that. They usually do what they say they are going to do, and they give as much as they take. Let's say you have a friend who usually shows up on time when you make commitments and is always there when you need someone to listen. However, lately, they haven't been themselves. They have canceled carefully made plans and seem to be generally "out of it" when you speak to them- one-word answers, not paying attention and you find yourself having to often repeat yourself to them, and even then they seem distracted, so you have to give up on what you're trying to tell them. Then you're having a stressful day, and you need to talk to someone, so you call them and they don't answer. This can be really frustrating, and since people have a tendency to personalize things, you might think they are doing this to spite you or to let you know they don't want to be your friend anymore. This is highly unlikely. If things have been going well between you and you can't think of any recent major arguments, it is pretty safe to assume you do not have anything to worry about on that front.

Many times, when your friend is suddenly not acting like themselves, it has nothing to do with you. They are not angry with you. In fact, they probably need you now more than ever, because it is very possible that they are going through something that is taking up all of their time. This often means a major life event. This could mean a death in the family, divorce, or loss of a job. In any of these cases, your friend is going through a time of great fear and is likely going through a depression. They might have broken commitments with you because they didn't feel like they had the emotional energy to do it, or because they didn't want to go out and be the downer that spoils the mood. That is the mindset a person has when they are stressed out and going through depression.

When a person is not on top of their game is when they need their friends the most, but it is not guaranteed that they will reach out to you first. They might not want to trouble. That is why we have a responsibility to be the ones to reach out to our friends when they are showing signs of being troubled. Take a look at your friend. You might notice they have lost weight and don't dress the way they usual, and are neglecting self-care.

You do not have to tell them you have noticed these things. In fact, it is ill-advised to do so because it might conjure up feelings of shame for them. Just tell them it has been a while since you two have last spoken, and you want to know if there's something you could do to help them. Do not ask them you have done something wrong or if they are angry with you. When a person is going through a stressful time, they do not need the added pressure of trying to reassure someone else.

Now that we have gotten to the part where they have told you what is going on, we will get into what to do to help them. You will need to take an active role in getting them out of their house and distracting them from their problems. It is a nice gesture to tell someone they can call you any time they need something from you or just to talk, but without follow-up, you won't hear from them. We as people have a self and society-imposed shame about telling someone we have a problem and asking for help about it. This is because we don't want to weigh other people down with the burdens we are carrying. We think they are already going through enough; they don't need me to add to their troubles. This is why you will need to be the one to reach out to them. Invite them to any kind of activity.

It is advisable to take them to something that requires either physical or mental activity, but not to the point where it is overwhelming. If you just take them to a movie, it will give them time to think about what is bothering them, not to mention there is the prospect of a scene coming up in the movie that reminds them of their trouble, making the outing counterproductive. Mini-golfing and bowling are a few good suggestions for what to invite them to. There is some activity required, but it isn't overwhelming, and it will help them get their mind off of things.

When we are helping a struggling loved one, we walk a thin line. On one hand, we need to always be ready to talk about it when they do, but on the other hand, we cannot push it. Sometimes they will start to talk about their problems, but then they might be overcome and then you will need to find a way to change the subject. It will be difficult to work through these transitions.

When you are an emotional caregiver, you need to be sure you are taking care of yourself too. It is said that every therapist needs their own therapist. This is because it takes a lot of energy from you to be consistently holding someone else. You might even start to get frustrated and tired, which is often referred to as caregiver burnout. You might even begin to suffer from something known as vicarious trauma, which is when you have been exposed to another person's trauma for a prolonged time, and it starts to affect you. Do not fight the emotions if you begin to have feelings of resentment. It is natural. While you care about the person and want to do everything you can to make them feel better, you are only human. There will be times where you have thoughts like, "It always has to be about them, it can never be about me." "I'm tired of walking on eggshells." "I thought things were getting better, and then today there was a relapse. Why does everything have to always be so heavy?"

These are valid feelings to have, and ones you need to have a place to vocalize. It needs to be somewhere private, where no one will hear this conversation. It needs to be with someone who realizes this is not you saying you are about to give up on the person, you just have some grievances you need to let out. If you do not do this, your feelings will not go away. They will fester, and if you bottle them up, at some point, you will explode, and it will likely be at a very inopportune. Understand that just because you have selfish feelings, doesn't mean you do not have empathy. This is where you exercise having empathy for yourself. Do not hold yourself to a standard where you never can have a human reaction to things, and you shouldn't browbeat yourself when you do.

When we have arguments with people, it is natural to go into the mode where you try to prove how you are right, and they are wrong. However, when we do this, we make barriers between us and the ones we care about because we are only thinking about what we want. You can stand your ground while still seeing your friend's side of things. Say they did not text you back, and that bothered you. You are entitled to your reaction to their lack of response and feeling upset with them about it, but you also need to consider why that might have happened. They might have been tired and couldn't respond to anyone. They also could have thought they responded and are unaware that they haven't. If we sink too deeply into our side of things, we will fail to see the true story because we make assumptions and refuse to listen to any other explanation.

The hardest thing you will ever have to do is admit when you have done wrong. Some people never get to that point, so you need to acknowledge the bravery you have shown when you show remorse for something you have done. It is not a sign of weakness or an admission of defeat. It is an acknowledgment that you are human and have made a mistake as we all do, the imperfect beings we are. Can you imagine how boring it would be if no one ever made a mistake? Not to mention, you would never grow.

An apology doesn't have to be long. In fact, it can come off as insincere if it goes on for too long. Do not do too much groveling. That can feel manipulative from the perspective of the other person. If you fill your apology with putdowns directed at yourself, they will feel the pressured to comfort you in a time that is supposed to be about them.

Also, do not say the words, "I'm sorry, but..." People do not tend to listen to what you say before the word "but," and they will feel like this is an insincere apology that was more of a way to earn sympathy or turn the situation around to be their fault. Either way, it will not be well-received. When you are giving an apology is not the time to give any grievances of your own. It is also not the time to make excuses.

"I said something inconsiderate to you, and I hurt your feelings when I said that. It isn't really what I feel, and I care about our relationship. I'm sorry, please forgive me." This is how simple an apology can and should be. If they do not accept your apology, you cannot force them to, and at this point, they are the ones who are being cruel. If they tell you they cannot forgive you and yet express an interest in maintaining the friendship, I caution you against taking them up on their offer. If you do, you will perpetually be paying for what you did, along with any other mistakes you make in the future. A relationship with an unforgiving person will make your life extremely difficult.

It is easy to see the people we love as people with valid opinions when all is going well, and there is no strife. You must remember the good times when you are having a disagreement with them. Empathy means having barriers you will not cross. This means no name-calling, no character assassination, and no outright insults. If someone crosses this barrier, it is no longer an argument, and it has become a devaluing situation. When we fall into a pattern of that with our loved ones, we have to stop.

Let's look at what the difference is between a normal argument and verbal abuse. In a normal argument, they are trying to convey genuine emotion. For example, "I don't like it when you continue working at the dinner table." They still love you, but they do have a grievance they want to share with the goal of working it out and improving the relationship, and thus, the two of you become closer. It becomes verbal abuse when they do not want to accomplish anything except to upset you by attacking your character or insulting your intelligence, for example, "You're selfish and ungrateful, and you can't even see that you are." This is only meant to be unkind.

Devaluing is the default way a person with narcissistic personality disorder fights. The goal is to tear down the other person's self-worth, and thus it creates a trauma bond. While you are going to have disagreements with your partner, it should not happen all the time, and your partner should never verbally abuse you. The narcissist insults belittle and go on tirades directed at their partner, and it is supposed to be intimidating. This is not a demonstration of love. This is not because they are so passionate. This is their personality disorder in action, and you cannot subject yourself to it. If a person is consistently verbally abusive to you, you must get out of the situation. It will not get better. It will only get worse. It is not unempathetic to leave an abuser. In fact, it is showing empathy to yourself by letting yourself know you are worth more than that.

Empathy also involves figuring out how to help your friend based on what you know about them. Earlier in the book, we discussed how different people are motivated by different incentives. The same concept applies when figuring out how to console a friend.

Think about how different people want different methods of care when they are physically ill. Some people want you to make a big deal out of it, while others do not want you to mention it. Some people want you to bring them soup, water, medicine, and blankets while commiserating with them about their pain. Others want to just be left alone so they can recover in peace.

When someone is suffering emotionally, they might be very vocal about it and want you to listen. They might cry and want you to hold them. Other people do not want to be treated that way because they are afraid of being seen as weak. For some people, sending them a card and caring for them from afar is the right way to go. Some people want someone to spend time with but do not want to talk about what is upsetting them, preferring a distraction. You must respect their wishes.

Even if your intentions are pure, you cannot try to force someone to talk about something. You might feel like it would be better for them to talk about how they feel so they can get their emotions out in the open and clear the air, but that might not be what they want to do. They might have been raised in a way that frowns upon that, so talking about emotions makes them feel uncomfortable. They also might not be ready to talk about what is bothering them. You cannot force a person to do something even if you feel like it would be good for them.

You also cannot change what other people are going to do. You might not like the decisions they are making, but the more you try to interfere, the more friction you will cause in your relationship with them. In fact, many times, when you try to discourage someone from doing something, that becomes all they want to do.

Advice is really something you are best off saving for when you are asked for it. If you give unsolicited advice, only give it once. Any more times than that and the person will feel at best annoyed and, at worst, persecuted. Most of the time, when a person is opening up to you about a problem they are going through, they just want someone to listen. You are most likely coming from a good place when you try to give them suggestions, but they can sometimes make the person feel like they are not being heard or like you are not interested in hearing what they have to say. If someone does not listen to your suggestions, you must let it go, even if they are sound ones.

Empathy involves connecting to people who are different from us and seeing that we are not as different as we think. As a benign example, imagine you are meeting someone who supports a sports team that rivals the one you are a fan of. Your first instinct might be that the two of you need to be rivals. However, is this really necessary? Obviously, both of you know that when it comes to game time, you will be cheering for opposite outcomes. That only has to happen over the course of the game, though. In your daily life, you can come to an understanding or even be friends. You might support different teams, but you have several similarities. Both of you are avid sports fans, and you know what it is like to feel a deep sense of pride in a certain team. This is a point where both of you can bond because you have an understanding of how the other feels about the team of their choice. You can find ways to talk about sports while navigating around the fact that you like different teams. You can come to an agreement where you will not speak badly about each other's favorite teams.

As another example, there are many circles of friends and even families where different members of the group support different political parties. This one is more difficult to navigate because politics is one of the most heated topics of discussion. People get passionate about it, and tempers can flare during these sorts of discussions. You need to really get to know yourself, your friend, and the relationship between the two of you so you can figure out whether or not you can discuss politics without things becoming inflammatory. If this is not possible, you should leave this topic out of your discussions. There are things you need to avoid talking about with certain friends because it will only lead to an unproductive conversation. You can agree to disagree.

You do not need to have the same views as someone about every issue in order for you to compatible with them as friends. You will probably never meet one person in your life with whom you are completely likeminded. In fact, you would probably become bored talking to this person even if you did meet them. That is what makes talking with people so interesting. We all come from different walks of life and therefore hold different opinions.

An empathetic person does not allow themselves to be walked on. However, they do understand that certain behaviors others exhibit might come with an explanation. Understanding a person is the way they are will make it easier for you to work with them. If you are going to be in a leadership role, you will need to understand how to deal with people who are difficult to work with.

When someone comes from a chaotic upbringing, there are a few ways this could impact their personality and the way they deal with other people. They might be confrontational and approach the world with a "get them before they get me" attitude. They might become easily offended, even if that was not your intention. They might be withdrawn and avoid conversations with people entirely. They might be shy and hesitant to assert themselves, being more concerned with not upsetting, which can make it very difficult to figure out what they are trying to say. They might not be able to handle much pressure or feel overwhelmed easily. They might not be good at taking criticism and become agitated when receiving it because they take it as a personal offense. In any of these cases, becoming angry is not going to anything but make a bad situation worse. If it is with a person who behaves confrontationally, getting angry at them will only make their temper worse, which will escalate into a yelling match, which will prove to be completely unproductive. If you lay into a person who is reserved and cannot handle much pressure, losing your temper with them is going to make them shut down and therefore be completely ineffective. A leader has to be able to reach people, even those who are a little more difficult to do so with.

Chapter 6:
Internal Motivation

We all know people who are self-starters and do not need a great deal of management to get a job done. The ability to motivate oneself into being productive makes a person a better student, employee, and friend. Again, this is an important component of leadership. Motivation is the driving force that keeps you going. It is the part of you that keeps going even when the cards are stacked against you. It ultimately needs to come from within, but there is nothing wrong with having outside factors that also motivate you.

Motivation is something everyone struggles with at some point, even the people who seem to be the most motivated ones you know. There are times you just don't want to do the things you have to do during the day. You feel uninspired and like everything is too much work. Motivation can be lost, but it can also be brought back.

The way you get out of bed sets a tone for the rest of your day. If you press the snooze button as many times as you can, you will have a feeling of being rushed for the rest of the day. This is because you are not confident in yourself as you walk out the door. You are not sure you have everything with you that you need, and you know you do not look your best. When you do not feel prepared, you will also feel tired. You will only want to get through the day and then go to bed as soon as possible.

If you stay up very late at night, you will not want to get up in the morning. Even if you sleep until late in the day, you will still feel groggy. You will do the bare minimum, and it will feel like you have to spend all of your strength to do it. If you need to get up early, it will be painful to get up, and it will be something you have to force yourself to do. You will be irritable throughout the day because you are running on so little sleep. Getting adequate rest is one of the foundational components of staying motivated. Trying to stay motivated without getting enough sleep would be like trying to keep a car going that had run out of fuel. It just won't work.

We cannot change the fact that we have responsibilities, and not all of them are ones we want to do. However, we can change the attitude we take on about them. Instead of dreading the next day because of what you will have to do, try looking forward to it because of what you will get to do. Is there a hobby you have wanted to try? Do it tomorrow. Give yourself something to look forward to, and then the days will feel like more than something you have to gut through.

Sometimes it is a little more than feeling tired or unmotivated. If it has been a long time since you felt enthusiastic about your own life, you might be going through a high-functioning form of depression and not know it. Do you feel like you have to just go through the motions of the day? Do you feel like nothing is terribly wrong, but nothing is going right, either?

Depression can be sneaky. You may not realize it is happening to you. There is a popular misconception that depression means you feel sad all the time. That's not quite it. Depression is more about the feelings of melancholy. You do not have any energy. You feel like there is something missing. Many people with depression report feeling numb and empty, and like they do not feel a sense of purpose.

Depression is a scary word for most people because they think it means being at risk for suicide. While it can happen, it is less likely than you would think. In fact, most people go through a time of depression at some point in their lives, particularly after a major life crisis. People who are going through a loss are particularly vulnerable to falling into a depression. Loss can be in the sense that they died, or it can also mean the loss of a relationship or even a friendship.

One of the most difficult things you will ever have to do is to pick yourself back up after you have suffered a loss. I will use the loss of a relationship as an example because it is one everyone will go through in some form, whether it is a breakup or a divorce. When something in your life is lost, it changes your entire life, especially if you lived with the person. Every detail of your day will be altered.

When they leave, make sure to fill up the space that is now vacant. It will be upsetting to see empty places where things of theirs used to be, and it will be a constant reminder of the breakup. For example, line up the clothes in your closet to where they are spaced out to make it not so obvious that their clothes are gone. Don't let there be a vacant side of your sink because your mind will go straight to the break up every time you see it.

First, maintain self-care. You will not want to do it because when you are struggling with depression. However, if you look good, it will help your mood. When you let yourself go outside looking haggard, it is like you are surrendering to the depression. Maintaining your physical health is important because it correlates with your mental health. You have to resist the urge to stay up late and then sleep all day because this could contribute to a depressed mode. This is because you will feel like you have wasted a day, which will kill your motivation. Try doing some form of workout in the morning. There are many workout tapes that are only 15 minutes long, making them easy to fit into your schedule. This will get your blood pumping, your body moving, and will give you a feeling of accomplishment. When you leave yourself enough time that you do not have to spring out of bed and immediately get to work, the tasks you need to complete for the day will not feel as daunting. They will also not feel like they drain all of your energy.

You also need to stay busy. When we are going through an emotionally painful time, we are likely to gravitate toward behaviors that are self-destructive when we are left to our own devices for too long. For instance, if you are alone in your house with your internet, you might start to become tempted to look up your former partner's social media profiles. This will only cause you pain. Instead of doing this, try thinking of something that needs to be done around the house. There might be a project you started a long time ago but never got off of the ground, likely because of the problems that were happening at home. Maybe you started playing an instrument, but it has been sitting in a closet unused. Maybe you started a painting or writing a story. There might be a yoga or other workout tape you bought but haven't opened yet. By going back to old projects, you rediscover yourself as well as channel your creativity.

You are at risk of subconsciously neglecting your other relationships when you lose one. You may not feel like going out and seeing anyone, but if you have too much time alone, you will have too much time to think about your breakup. Do not listen to anyone who tells you there is a certain amount of time you have to spend by yourself before getting back out there and dating again. There is nothing good that comes from spending too much time alone. As a disclaimer, this does not mean you have to find another relationship and make a deep commitment to it right away. This means go out on some dates. If someone invites you to get coffee, do it.

When people are getting out of a long-term relationship, it will sometimes take them a while to really register that they are single. They will turn down potential opportunities to meet people because it doesn't feel right. The only person it needs to feel right to is you. Remember, in the end; it is you who has to stay with or away from a person. You are the one who will be feeling the effects of it. You will not get anything out of making a decision you don't want to in order to please someone else or because they find fault with what you want to do. If you do meet someone shortly after a breakup and you click with them, there is no reason for you not to start a relationship with them.

You will never be as motivated as when you are using the right things as your incentives. If your motivations come from an external place, it will feel like a burden you have to bear. If your motivation is your own happiness, you will feel a spark of energy within you. This is not a bad thing. There are certain times where it is good to be selfish. When it will not come at a strong personal cost to other people, but will help you, be selfish.

Part of your motivation comes from the people you surround yourself with. The people we have in our lives affect our behavior and habits. If you spend time with people who have a negative outlook on life and do not wish to better themselves, their attitude will take a toll on you. They will prohibit you from living up to your full potential.

 An example of this kind of person wants you to skip school. This means they want to take you away from your education and away from self-improvement. It also shows that they are not concerned about the prospect of you being caught and getting into trouble. They might speak badly about the people who go to their classes. You cannot let this person be a motivational force in your life.

You want to spend your time with the people who encourage you to go to your classes and who will help you study for your tests. You want to be around the people who are involved in clubs and are proud of this fact.

It might be true that the person who wants you to skip school is having challenges at home. You can feel compassion for them, and you can encourage them to get help with their situations, but you cannot let yourself be brought down by them. If they do not wish to get help, that is their decision. Your choice of friends is an extremely important one. You cannot choose people who are going to bring you down. There is a level of closeness you can keep people's problems, and closer than that is unhealthy. You need to hold them at arm's length. You can be invested in them and do what is in your power to help them, but you do not want to lose sleep over it. You also do not want to try to do things you do not really have the power to do.

In order to get motivated, you need to set goals for yourself. One of the reasons people can fall into a rut of being unproductive is that they feel aimless in what they are doing. If you do not feel like you are working towards something, you will not work as hard. Set goals for yourself each day. They do not have to be the be-all and end-all goals. Just figure out what you need to get done today while you are working towards your ultimate goals.

You also need to understand that motivation has an ebb and flow. Some days you are more motivated than others, and that is okay. Let's say you are writing an essay, and the time you have to do it versus the words you need to write adds up to writing 500 words per day. There will be days you can go beyond that quota and get ahead of schedule. There will be other days where it will be all you can do just to get those 500 words written. There is nothing wrong with you for having days like that. Sometimes you will just be tired. These times tend to come when you have been working long hours lately, and you need to give yourself permission to relax and do the bare minimum on those days. Relaxing might be what you need to do to get your inspiration and energy back so you can be hard at work again soon. There is getting the most out of your day, and then there is pushing yourself too hard. If you do the latter, you might actually wind up being less productive than if you had just given yourself a break.

People who have just recently graduated from college often struggle with finding motivation, so if this is happening to you, you are far from being alone. It is a tough transition going from school to the next chapter of your life. Sometimes people feel lost. You have worked for at least four years toward getting this degree, and then what do you do with it? The answer is not always immediate, and there are many college graduates who are dealing with feelings of shame and anxiety as a result of not knowing what to do next. You have placed an expectation on yourself to land a job in the field you earned your degree in shortly after graduation.

It takes many college graduates at least a year to find a job. For some, it is even two years, and some people take even longer. You haven't failed just because you haven't followed the same paths as others. You have your own life to figure out, and doing it sooner or later than other people does not make you any better or worse than anyone else. You need to find your own path and do not let anyone else make you feel bad about what you have or have not done.

During the time where you are job hunting after graduation, keeping your motivation up is more important than ever. It can get discouraging because you are going to get a lot of rejections before you manage to get your foot in the door. It is not uncommon for this to discourage people to the point where they become lax in their sending out applications for jobs. This will only make more days pass by with nothing to show for it. First, it is extremely important that you resist the urge to sleep in until the afternoon. This is a part of depression. It is also a way to get out of job searching for the day because, by the time you get up and around, you can tell yourself it is too late in the day to do anything about it now. You tell yourself this is the last day this happens and tomorrow you will be up at six in the morning putting in more applications than anyone ever has before, but then tomorrow comes, and you end up first falling asleep at six in the morning, and the same cycle repeats itself.

If this is happening to you right now, this is what you need to do. Go to bed early tonight. You cannot function without a good night's sleep. Sleeping until two in the afternoon after falling asleep at four doesn't cut it. You will wake up and feel just as tired as you did before you went to sleep because our bodies are not meant to have that type of sleep cycle. Taking melatonin is helpful because it is a natural sleep aid and will lull you to sleep instead of knocking you out. When you intend to fall asleep, put away everything that could distract you. Put away your phone, computer, and any other electronic device. Do not contact anyone anymore. This will keep you awake.

You also need to turn off the TV in order to avoid falling into the trap where you promise yourself you are just going to watch one more episode of a show, but that one comes to an end so you decide since it's already a disturbing hour of the morning you might as well watch another one. Lie down and turn the lights off. If putting on relaxing music helps you, do it. Do whatever helps you sleep, and put all of your worries away for tomorrow. You cannot do anything about them now, and you will not be able to do anything about them tomorrow if you get poor sleep. Some people visualize a place they go to in their minds to relax and put away their problems. It can be anything you want, whether it is a cabin in the middle of the snowy forest or a resort on the beach or even a fantasy world. The only thing it must be is somewhere that makes you happy and feel relaxed. You will fall asleep much faster if you are free of distractions and not thinking about anything that has the potential to cause you anxiety.

You'll be surprised at how much more refreshed you feel waking up after a good night's rest. This is because your body has gotten the first bit of good sleep it has in a long time. You don't get quality sleep when you pass out at some hour of the morning out of sheer exhaustion. However, when you wake up in the morning after sleeping at a reasonable hour, you will feel better not only physically but emotionally and mentally as well. When you are deprived of sleep, your mood goes down. Your decision-making skills are impaired, and your emotions run higher than usual. This means you are more likely to cry or get angry, which only compounds your problems because you are already feeling a large amount of stress about your unemployment. You do not have much stamina, which will impair your ability to go job hunting. It will seem like too much work, causing you to take a look at the application and decide there is too much to do for it, and then leave the page. When you are well-rested, your mood is more neutral, and you feel like you are ready to take on the day.

Create a morning ritual for yourself. Have some coffee, and make yourself some breakfast. Eggs are great for cognitive function. Take a bath or shower and use scents that promote liveliness. A morning ritual will make your world not seem so small and like you aren't stuck in a situation where all you do is work. Make yourself look put-together. If you are lounging around in your pajamas, you will feel less motivated.

Now, here comes the hard part, which is the job-hunting part. There is a saying that goes, "if you do not have a job, your job is finding one." You will need to send a large number of applications per day. Make a set number for yourself and stick to that quota. If you keep on applying, something will happen.

A problem that often stifles people is looking for entry-level jobs and finding that the requirements include something like "5 years of experience in marketing" or something to that effect. This is likely because someone is copying and pasting on the ads and not looking at what they are posting. If they are listing it as an entry-level job and not going to pay for someone with that type of experience, they should not insist on someone with that type of experience. Apply anyways.

While you are job hunting, make sure you do not neglect other aspects of your life. Spend time with friends and family. You will need the support of others through this difficult time. You should also indulge in your hobbies. You do not need to spend every single second of your day looking at job postings. In fact, that is a way to get burned out quickly. You need things to do that lift up your mood because this is going to be a depressing time at first.

Motivation can run low when you are thinking about the things you do not have. That is why you need to build up your optimism. We can often find ourselves in a place where we are thinking, "If I just had the job I wanted," or "If only I had more friends or a boyfriend/girlfriend." Whatever it is, fill in the blank and end the sentence with, "then I would be happy." Happiness cannot rely on an external source; otherwise, it will only come to you in short bursts and be torn down easily. Disappointments will be unbearable.

Think about how you feel when you wake up in the morning. You are in a bed with blankets keeping you warm. You are in a heated or air-conditioned house, so you are not exposed to the elements. You have food in the fridge and a shower. Those are all things to be grateful for because not everyone in the world has these things. If you do not have your dream job, that can still be achieved. If you do not have as many friends as you would like or a romantic relationship, you have the means to change that.

A motivation killer for many people is feeling like they are too young or old to do something. That sense of it being too late to chase your dreams is a depressing one. It is also a useless thought because it is not true. If you have an idea, you need to explore it. Not every actor was in their twenties when they got started; in fact, some of them were in their fifties or even later. There are people who published their first book when they were 90 years old. Just because you do not start as early as some people doesn't mean you are too late. It is only too late when your life is over. Until then, anything is possible. Lamenting about the things that haven't happened yet will do no good for you. Think about where you want to be in the future, but most importantly, think about the present.

Another thing you need to watch out for is the temptation to lose motivation when you run into a setback. Say you have written a book and are trying to get it published. You have been working on the book for months, maybe even years. You are filled with a sense of accomplishment upon having written the final page. This feeling of confidence is soon replaced with dread when you realize now it is time to try to find a way to get it published. You send it to a few publishing agencies and get a rejection note from them. You start to lose hope and wonder if what you have to say just isn't what anyone else wants to hear. This is the time where you think about how far you have come. It would be a tragedy if you gave up now. Read the stories of famous authors and how many times they were rejected before they got their foot in the door.

Sometimes motivation doesn't come in the form of this fire within you that burns with a passion, making you feel like you are capable of anything. Sometimes it is when you are at your lowest point, and you feel like nothing is possible. It is when you feel like giving up, but then something inside you says, "just keep going." Sometimes motivation comes in the form of just getting through another day and doing the things you need to do to keep going. Remember that a bad day is nothing more than that: a bad day. The next day will come along and with it another opportunity. If you didn't do your best today, leave that in the past. The day that is coming up is a new beginning. Forgive yourself for whatever mistakes you feel you have made and then keep going. Motivation is putting one foot in front of the other even when you do not feel like it.

Keep a positive thought about yourself. That is the core of motivation. Do not feel bad about yourself when you fail. Sometimes it is not your fault when things go wrong, and even if it is, recognize that you are human and, therefore, will make mistakes. Strive to do better in the future and then move on.

CONCLUSION

So much of communication is perception. We need to understand how we feel and really be in touch with ourselves in an honest way. A person who can do this and also keep control of their own emotions will more effectively understand others and communicate in a healthier way. By understanding the components of emotional intelligence, we can train ourselves to utilize its tools and components to smooth our way in life. By truly listening to others and being observant of their nonverbal cues as well as being mindful of our place in the social circle, we can avoid miscommunication and damages to relationships.

Others find great comfort when they feel they are understood and empathized with. It brings a sense of closeness when we feel that we others have put themselves in our shoes, so it's important to mirror this action to others in return. Behaving with a sense of compassion is important along with assuming that the other person has good intentions. It is very important to remember this without jumping to conclusions and acting negatively without thinking. A person who can regulate themselves influences how a difficult conversation goes. We cannot remove all conflict from life, but we can manage our own personal reactions.

The more often we practice emotional intelligence, the better our relationships work, and the more positively we are seen in society. People who exhibit emotional intelligence are seen as leaders, and it can lead to more opportunities for advancement at work as well as other civic opportunities in your community. Emotional intelligence most certainly improves any and all interpersonal relationships.